What's for lunch?

Milk

Library of Congress Cataloging-in-Publication Data
Llewellyn, Claire.
    Milk / Claire Llewellyn.
    p.   cm. -- (What's for lunch?)
    Includes index.
    Summary: Tells the story of milk from the time it is taken from the cow
on the diary farm through to its processing and distribution to users.
    ISBN 0-516-20840-3
    1. Milk --Juvenile literature. 2. Diarying--Juvenile
literature. 3. Dairy products--Juvenile literature. [1. Milk. 2. Dairying.
3. Dairy products.] I. Title. II. Series.
Llewellyn, Claire. What's for Lunch?
SF239.5. L58 1998   97-39803
641.3'71--dc21   CIP
                                                AC

First American edition 1998 by
Franklin Watts
A Division of Grolier Publishing
Sherman Turnpike
Danbury, CT 06816

ISBN   0-516-20840-3 (lib. bdg.)
ISBN   0-516-26221-1 (pbk)

Editor: Samantha Armstrong
Series Designer: Kirstie Billingham
Consultant: National Dairy Council.
Reading Consultant: Prue Goodwin, Reading and Language
Information Centre, Reading.

Printed in Hong Kong

What's for lunch?

Milk

Claire Llewellyn

CHILDREN'S PRESS®

A Division of Grolier Publishing

NEW YORK • LONDON • HONG KONG • SYDNEY
DANBURY, CONNECTICUT

Today we are drinking milk with our lunch.
Milk is full of goodness.
It contains **proteins**, **vitamins**, and **minerals**.
Milk gives us **energy** and helps us grow
and stay healthy.

Most of the milk we drink
comes from cows on **dairy farms**.
Cows feed on grass, so dairy farms
are found in places where the grass grows
juicy and thick.

Cows are **mammals,**
and, like all mammals,
they feed their young
milk.

After giving birth to a calf,
a cow produces milk
in her **udder.**

She makes much more
than her calf needs.

We take some of the milk
and use it for ourselves.

Cows spend most of the year **grazing** in fields. When the weather gets cold, the grass stops growing, and the cows are brought into a large cowshed. There they are fed **hay,** **cereals,** and other kinds of food.

hay

Cows are usually milked twice a day -
once in the early morning
and again in the afternoon.
They are milked in a **milking parlor**.
Their udders are washed and dried
and then covered by four **teat cups**.
These squeeze the cows' udders very gently
and draw the milk into a container.

The milk is piped into a large, clean
storage tank called a **farm vat**.
The vat is **refrigerated** to keep the milk cool.

After milking, the farmer hoses down the parlor with water and makes sure that everything is spotlessly clean.

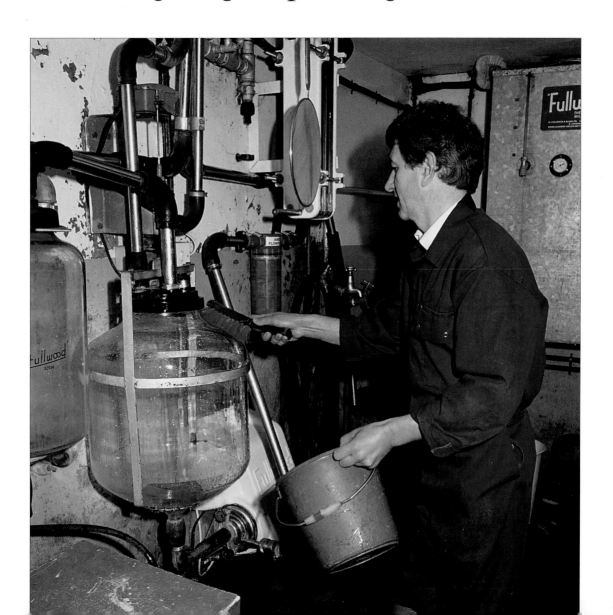

Every morning a tanker comes to collect the milk.
The driver connects a long hose to the vat, and
the milk is sucked up into the tanker.
The driver transports the milk to the **dairy**.

At the dairy, the milk is
specially treated to keep it fresh.
This treatment is called **pasteurization**.
Pasteurization is important
because it kills **bacteria**
that could harm us.

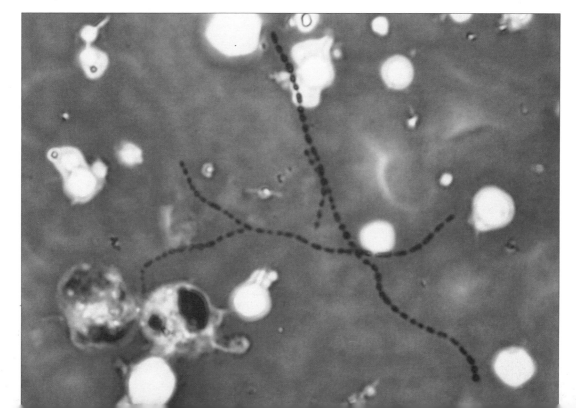

Cows' milk is very creamy.
Some people like all the cream
in their milk; some like just a little;
and others prefer none at all.
At the dairy, the cream can be
skimmed off to make
low-fat milk and skim milk.
The milk is put into different
colored cartons.

The cartons are loaded onto trucks.
The trucks are refrigerated to keep
the milk fresh.
They deliver the milk to stores
for people to buy.

Not all milk ends up in cartons.
Some of it is delivered to factories
called **creameries**, where butter
and different types of cheese are made.

Some milk is used to make yogurt.
Frozen cream is used
to make ice cream.
Sometimes fruit and other flavors
are added to give yogurt and
ice cream delicious tastes.

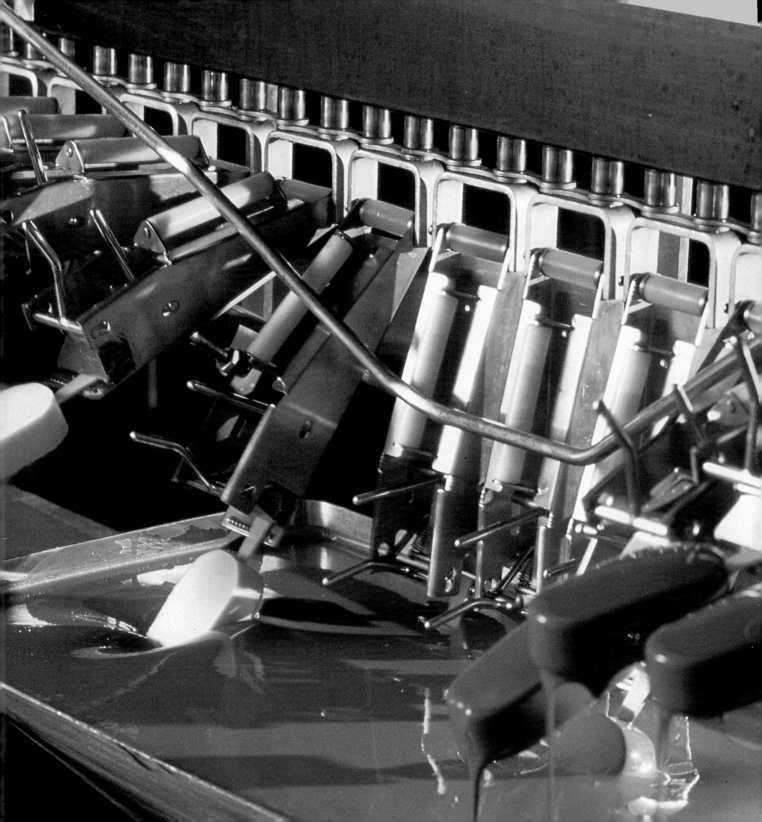

We use milk to make sauces,
pancakes, and puddings.
We also use it for milk shakes.
See how many ways you enjoy
milk every day!

Glossary

bacteria   tiny living things that exist all around us and can cause disease

cereal   a kind of plant, such as wheat, oats, and barley, that is grown for its grains

creamery   a factory in which cheese and butter are made

dairy   a place where milk is processed

dairy farms   farms where cows are raised for their milk

energy   the strength to work and play

farm vat   a large container where milk is kept

graze   to feed on grass outside in fields

hay   dried grass

mammal   an animal, such as a cow, that gives birth to its young and feeds it milk

milking parlor   the place where cows are taken to be milked

mineral	a material that is found in rocks and also in our food. Minerals are important for a healthy body
pasteurization	a way of heat treating milk that destroys harmful bacteria
protein	something found in foods, such as milk and meat, that helps build our body and keep us healthy
refrigerate	make cool
skimmed	milk from which the cream has been removed
teat cups	suction cups that gently squeeze the milk from the cow's udder
udder	the part of the cow where milk is stored
vitamin	something found in food, especially milk, fruits, and vegetables, that keeps us healthy

Index

Picture credits: Bruce Coleman (Hans Reinhard) 8-9; Eye Ubiquitous (David Langfield) 21, 22; FLPA (Peter Dean) 6, 7, 10-11, 14, 15; Holt Studios International 13 (Nigel Cattlin), 24 (Inga Spence); Image Bank 16-17, 18 (Francesco Anggeri), 27 (Juan Silva); Oxford Scientific Films 19; Steve Shott cover; All other photographs Tim Ridley, Wells Street Studios, London. **With thanks to Roxanne Carney and Thomas Ong.**